Lifeline
A devotional journey

Tiffany Garigan

To: Kathy
Merry Christmas!

ACKNOWLEDGEMENTS

First, I must pay respect to God, who performed this extraordinary miracle in my life. Next, I have to acknowledge my mother, who stopped her life, to step in for mine. Now, I must thank my father and sister for their undying love and commitment throughout my recovery and journey. Without each one, I would have lacked love, care, and support needed to carry me through each day.

Day 1

Turn to the wall

Isaiah 38:2 NIV

On March 20, 2012, I was rushed to the hospital by ambulance, nearly lifeless. In fact, so lifeless, I do not even remember. Resuscitation started in the ambulance, then again at the hospital. My family soon arrived.

Once they arrived, the information they received was that I only had two hours to live. My diagnosis was a pulmonary embolism that began in my legs and traveled to my lungs. During the time of waiting, my mother consistently prayed as family and friends began pouring into the hospital waiting area. One of the many ways she told me she waited was turning her face to the wall and praying to God as Hezekiah did.

Isaiah 38:2 NIV

Then Hezekiah turned his face to the wall and prayed to the Lord.

The wall Hezekiah turned to was a literal wall. This very act shows the need for seclusion. Hezekiah spent this time literally crying out to God with flowing tears. His prayer was to remind God, even though God did not need reminding, that he was faithful and served Him truthfully. Hezekiah knew he could call on God even at the time of death.

Hezekiah turned to the wall, not because of fear or shame. He turned to the wall to dismiss all distractions. He knew the request to not meet death had to be made with intention.

Daily application

Take a moment to clear yourself of any distractions and be intentional about hearing from God. God hears all request whether they are bold or not. My mother made a bold request, just like Hezekiah. Today I challenge you to clear your space to only you and God. Once you do so, be bold about your needs, and watch Him work.

Day 2

Your presence is enough

Genesis 28:15 ESV

Doctors did not think I had a chance of living through the first night, however, if I did, I had a chance at life again, a limited life, but life, nonetheless. The next day came around; I was still alive and continuously fighting. I had a feeding tube and remained incapacitated. In the midst of all of this, God remained present.

God made a promise to keep me through all things. His presence permeated the hospital atmosphere like no other. Anything that God promises must happen, and His word will never return void. Even though things did not look like God was present, He was. God kept me here to fulfill His plan for my life. In order to fulfill His divine plan; He required all of my attention. The thing He did to acquire it had just began to take place.

Genesis 28:15 ESV

Behold I am with you and will keep you wherever you go and will bring you back into this land, for I will not leave you until I have done what I have promised you

God had a set of promises specifically tailored for Jacob. God sent Jacob to spread seed throughout the land, this seed is God's word. This promise is a big deal because God sent Him out into all of the land, even land where he was prone to rejection. All Jacob needed was the word God promised him; this was that He would be with him wherever he went.

This word applied to me because God sent me out into a land that I had no idea how to navigate on my own. I did not have the tools to remove myself from life support, nor did I have the tools to navigate the obstacles that were ahead of me.

Daily Application

As your day progresses, understand that God's presence is all you need to make it through. If you do not sense God's presence for whatever reason, all you need to do is simply yearn for it, and He will surely reign down. Remember, God's word will never return void and He is a promise keeper.

Day 3

Ordered steps

Psalms 37:23 AMP

A few days in, I awoke without eyesight. I went blind, completely blind. My mom asked if I could see her during a conversation because I consistently looked in other directions. When she asked this question, we both realized I could not see and burst into tears. Why on earth would God allow this to happen? My progression was clear because I was taken off life support. I sang "order my steps, in your name dear Lord" often. I had no doubt that my steps were ordered by God, but what happens when He orders steps backward? This is not the only instance my steps were ordered, what seemed to be backward.

Psalms 37:23 AMP

The steps of a good and righteous man are directed and established by the Lord.

Righteous means to be commendable, deserving, or upright. The fight I already put up early on was a peek into how determined and dedicated I would be to the fight that lay ahead. I proved to God and myself that I was ready for battle.

Regardless, of what may occur in life, God's provision and protection will remain. This thing that happened to me, as awful as it is in the natural, is a part of the God ordered steps for my life.

Daily Application

Being counted righteous is not something solely kept for those in high positions, even though the word alone seems to give off this vibe. To be counted righteous, all you have to do is be focused, committed and dedicated to the task God has put before you.

Once your commitment to the steps God has ordered for your journey blossoms, then you will be counted righteous. Throughout this day, pay close attention to the things you do, analyze them and determine if they are pleasing to God.

Make it a strong habit to take self-inventory and purposely order your steps to align with God's daily will for you. Understand, even when your progress seems to be at a standstill or going backwards does not mean that God is not present or did not order that standstill

Day 4

My assignment

Luke 12:48 KJV

By this time, I was moved to another hospital where I began more rigorous inpatient therapy, while still blind and weak. Recovery came up to a place where I was able to put forth more effort. God had already given me much by giving me life again. Now, I was on the brink of a new chapter that required more of me, mentally, spiritually and physically.

Now, it is obvious that I received very much. Not only was I given a great portion in the natural, but there was also a lot of promises set aside for me to be awarded based on my faith and perseverance in the days ahead. Eventually, I became aware of my exact condition, I remember days of continuous tears and emotional pain.

Each day nurses and therapists would get me up and fill in the spaces of things I was unable to do. They would bathe me, alongside my mom, dress me, and feed me. Every time I had therapy, more of my own strength was required. As every day passed, I was able to do more than the previous.

Luke 12:48 KJV

To whom much is given, much is required.

To whom much is given, much is required means to me that the more God gives to me, and trusts me with, the more I am required to give to Him regardless of my personal feelings. I had to learn to steer away from myself. This was hard on so many levels. It was not only my duty to give back to Him directly, but also give to His people the testimony of all the miracles He performed. Even though my job was not clear yet, my journey as an ambassador for Christ began, right there in that very hospital room.

Daily Application

Think about what God has given you and examine if you have given Him the return He deserves. Wouldn't you want what you have given to someone to be reciprocated?

Day 5

God will not leave you undone

Mark 8:23-25 KJV

I made it to a victory point. I could see, not 20/20, but I could see. One of the first moments I remember as my vision gradually returned was sensing light. Everything appeared like looking through wax paper. Time moved forward and more touching came about.

I was eventually able to see clearly. First, the ability to sense the direction of light came about. Next, the ability to see straight ahead came and eventually my peripheral vision began slowly to fill in. To this day, it is continuing to heal.

Mark 8:23-25 KJV

And He took the blind man by the hand and led him out of the town, and when He had spit on his eyes and put His hands upon him, He asked him if he could saw ought. And he looked up and said, I see men as trees walking. After that, He put his hands again upon his eyes and made him look up, and he was restored and saw every man clearly.

Do not let the first touch discourage you if the results are not what you want. This could be a sign that your faith is continuing to develop.

Daily Application

Allow God to touch you more than once. Activate your faith. Divine healing and supernatural intervention could be at stake.

__Day 6__

A renewed mind

Romans 12:2 KJV

When I recognized my eyesight began to come back, I felt a sense of wholeness again. The ability to see did not define me. However, it did provide comfort and confirmation God was still present.

My vision healed, my speech got better, still unclear, but better. In addition, my walking strengthened; I was able to take a few steps at a time.

Visualization took place. Even though I did not understand what was going on. The only way I saw myself and the situation was as a loss at that time. The thoughts I had only focused on what I missed and not what I regained. I failed to look at my circumstances as another lesson on this journey.

At the beginning of life development, our minds are not in a phase where we understand the toughness of learning mobility. It is a natural born process. When these abilities were taken away from me, I had no idea how I would get further in life. The life I was accustomed to, no longer exist.

Romans 12:2 KJV

And be not conformed to this world: but be ye transformed by the renewing of your mind, that ye may prove what is that good and acceptable, and perfect, will of God.

In this text, God is giving us clear directions on how not to resemble or replicate the state of this world. Had my thoughts aligned with the medical reports I received, I would still be here today, because it is God's will. However, I would be carrying an unnecessary load of negative, worldly thinking.

Daily Application

Spend time committing to complete mental renewal. Allot dedicated quiet time for yourself and God. The only thing He needs from you is your desire to have a renewed mind. A mind transformed into God will only return in benefits.

Day 7

Open my eyes

Philippians 4:8 NIV

My vision became clearer over time. However, my eyes were also opened to something more. The realness of God. It is one thing to know biblical stories and someone who God healed. A different type of experience occurs when it is you. If I had to choose this encounter for myself, I can honestly say that I would not. I mean who would choose to go blind after a full life of seeing? Not me.

This journey was not up to me. God handpicked me, and He did so for a specific reason. Whatever the reason, it can only be fulfilled through Him.

What did I see when my spiritual eyes were opened? A love so pure, that it is unexplainable. The amazing part is, it has always been available. God simply waited on me to yearn for it truthfully and whole-heartedly.

Opening my eyes in this sense required me to open my heart and mind, even in that hard place of not knowing anything. One thing I finally came to the knowledge of is that I had to undergo a transformation and it had to start with me being committed.

These trials were not an easy phase to think about things noble, right, lovely, and pure.

Not only did I have to think about these things, but I also had to put my Godly vision on and see these things too.

Philippians 4:8 NIV

Finally, brothers and sisters, whatever is true, whatever is noble, whatever is right, whatever is pure, whatever is lovely, whatever is admirable, if anything is excellent or praiseworthy, think about such things.

Paul is spending time talking to the Philippians in this section. He is telling them to focus their attention only on the ways of God understand better days are ahead.

Daily application

Align your thoughts with Gods. Take the time to inventory your feelings and views of any circumstance. If an ungodly thought comes to your mind, be intentional about pulling it down.

Day 8

Faith in action

James 2:26 KJV

After I learned to consistently think on the ways of God, I needed to put them into action. Even though my vision slowly returned, it still was not clear enough nor strong enough for everything, specifically drive. My peripheral vision had gaps in it that seemed permanent to my doctor. After I completed a series of eye exams, the eye doctor came in the exam room, she told me I would never be able to drive again, there is no help for my vision, and I did not need to come back. Immediately I burst into tears and proclaimed loudly in the doctor's office, "I do not receive that," the doctor then exited the room. My family and I followed. We checked out of the doctor's office and returned home.

I know the doctor was doing her job. Based on the exam results, I was not supposed to be behind the wheel. What she did not know was where God brought me from and what was next for me. Eventually I was comforted and realized it was time for me to activate more faith.

For so long, the prayers and faith of others, specifically my mother, filled the gaps when I was unable to go to God's throne myself.

God is a God of action. I spent time with Him and even understood His teachings. This time came when I had to put into practice the lessons I learned. This chance was when I received the results of this eye exam. Faith in action can be rebuking negativity or taking steps to reach a goal. As long as you put forth some effort consistently, God will always meet you where you are and do what you cannot.

James 2:26 KJV

For as the body without the spirit is dead, faith without works is dead also.

Faith is an action word.

Daily application

Put your faith in action and make bold declarations. Take the time to journal something

God is calling you to make a bold declaration over.

Day 9

Clear the room

Mark 5:39 NIV

God needed my space clear. The first instance of space clearing occurred at the beginning of my hospital stay in March 2012. One of the doctors commanded that I have no more visitors because I needed rest.

Later, I began to spend more time alone as therapy ended and my family returned to work.

This situation of clearing was not like March 2012. I approached another crossroad that required only God and me. My space was cleared. I was no longer around family, friends, and co-workers like before and the visits and calls began to dwindle down. My room was cleared. The point of death passed away, but another point in recovery was upon me.

My space, or what I referred to as my "room" had to remain clear. I had zero room for naysayers, even the medical professionals, who were doing their jobs and gave me diagnosis' based on medical research and patient experiences and no room for idleness.

My anticipation of death was not actual death. After all, the physical death happened while I was on life support when I was unaware of my situation. This new season was marked by a death to anything not of God. I only fed myself with positive and productive conversations, situations, and surroundings. Since my direction was changing, I had to change with it.

Mark 5:39 NIV

God went in and said to them, "Why all this commotion and wailing? The child is not dead but asleep?"

Stop your mourning and rejoice, everything is not always, what it seems.

Daily application

What does your room need to be cleared from to receive your miracle? Take time to clear your space to hear from God. If you feel uncertain about His direction, press into him for clarity.

__Day 10__

Steadfast

1 Corinthians 15:58 ESV

Days in in-patient rehabilitation were not pleasant, once I realized I was there. The staff was nice, but my emotions were all over the place when I was not sleeping. Everyday my mom fed me breakfast, bathed me, brushed my hair, clothed me, brushed my teeth, put on my shoes, and tied them to prepare me for therapy. When therapy time came, I was loaded into my wheelchair and began the day with my speech, physical and occupational therapists.

These days seemed so long, when I started out, I could barely move, my motions were limited, I could not roll myself over in bed or sit up without any aid. Another level of root deepening was upon me. Now that I began to do more with help, I had to remain planted in God and understand that none of my work was in vain. Sometimes it felt like it was. I had to make myself aware that there was a bigger picture and set my focus on it. God is the author of the bigger picture, not me. I only had to set my sights and mind on the fact that there was a much larger plan and I had no control over it.

1 Corinthians 15:58 ESV

Therefore, my beloved brothers, be steadfast, immovable, always abounding in the work of the Lord, knowing that in the Lord, your labor is not in vain.

This season taught me the real lesson in this scripture. I was living it. Each day when I arose to therapy, I had no other choice than to take on the day rooted in the promises of God. His promises made me rich, abound, and fully equipped to tackle the day.

Daily application

What is God calling you to remain steadfast and immovable in? Do you trust Him enough to remain steadfast on His timeline even if you have to start over?

Day 11

Send a word

Matthew 6:8-13 KJV

Among everything I was going through, I also had seizures. Seizures and low mobility, not exactly the combination I was looking for. Each time my body experienced a seizure, a full tingling sensation took over me entirely. Similar to the feeling of when your foot falls asleep.

Each time I had a seizure, my mother said the Lord's Prayer and they stopped! Imagine the power of a word. When God's word goes forth, the storm has to cease, even an electrical brainstorm.

Matthew 6:8-13 KJV

Be not ye therefore like unto them: for your Father knoweth what things you have need of before you ask Him. After this manner therefore pray ye: Our Father which art in Heaven, hallowed be thy name. Thy kingdom come. Thy will be done in earth as it is in heaven. Give us this day our daily bread: and forgive us our debts, as we forgive our debtors. And lead us not into temptation, but deliver us from evil: For thine is the kingdom, and the power, and the glory, forever. Amen.

A few years in, I wondered how on earth do the Lord's Prayer and seizures relate.

The portion of this prayer regarding my seizures that stood out to me was, give us this day, our daily bread. My daily bread in those moments was God stopping my seizures.

Daily application

You need something from God on this day. Seek Him in prayer. Reverence and acknowledge His will and ways. Whatever your daily bread is, He will surely provide.

Day 12

The reward is coming

Galatians 6:9 ESV

Seasons came and went. Another new phase was upon me now. I was transitioning from the hospital to home. I will admit; I was afraid. Most people would be eager to go home; I was not. I grew comfortable with around the clock medical attention, even though getting sleep throughout the night was hard. The hospital became a safe place. I knew nurses, doctors, therapists, and staff would always be in and out. Days in therapy were hard and some had tears. Each day my therapists reassured me that if I put in the work, the dedication would soon show.

Well, this accomplishment was now upon me. Being released to go home from the hospital was a reward, regardless of my views. It is a graduation from one level to the next. Rewarding yet still challenging was the way I began to look at things. Home is a place I knew, but I had to become re-acquainted with it. My mobility was different now and my vision was low. I had to navigate a familiar place with unfamiliar circumstances.

I did not faint in this season, as the scripture says not to do. Instead, I stayed the course and reaped the benefits of graduating to a new phase. Performing well as unto God comes with countless benefits. This does not mean the uphill climb will be easy, but it will definitely be worth it.

Galatians 6:9 ESV

And let us not grow weary in well doing, for in due season, we will reap, if we faint not.

I reaped the reward of transition. Staying the course was my primary focus. Fear had no place with me, fear also comes with zero reward, I felt the fear and moved forward anyhow.

In this text, Paul is addressing the Galatians and warns them that trusting their own ways leads to self-destruction. If I failed to trust God during this transition and after, my reward could have passed me by.

Daily application

Today, journal parts of your life where there is great reward if you do not grow weary.

Day 13

The game plan

Jeremiah 29:11 NIV

God never intended to hurt me throughout this process, even though much of it was extremely hard. His pruning process is very much different from anything I would have ever imagined. I have gone through many fires and flames on this journey. Just like the Hebrew boys, Shadrach, Meshach, and Abednego, I came out unburnt and unscathed because God has been with me every step of the way (Daniel 6). Everyday, I am intentional about inviting God into my life.

His plans for my life are far greater than anything I can imagine or do for myself. His game plan became my game plan. All I did was follow His lead. After all, God knows the plans He has for me.

Jeremiah 29:11 NIV

For I know the plans I have for you declares the Lord, plans to prosper you and not to harm you, plans to give you hope and a future.

Jeremiah the prophet sends a letter to survivors who endured being in exile under King Nebuchadnezzar with clear directions. To the people who dwelled on the land the circumstances were undesirable. God uses Jeremiah as a messenger to send His words of comfort.

For me, my situation was undesirable. The more I grew in God; I understood this verse and chapter in context. God does know the plans He has for me; my job was to completely relax.

In other words, God is saying, "I got you!"

Daily application

The heavenly plan already exists for your life. Do your part to gain access to it. The plan is only waiting on you. Put your obedience into action. You may feel like you are in some form of entrapment now, it is only for a season, God has a plan for you.

Day 14

Keep Walking

Deuteronomy 29:3-6 NIV

I always only wanted the bigger picture, the end result. In addition, I only wanted my version to be the outcome and I wanted it on my time, immediately. Growth in this area reminds me of the account of the children in the wilderness for forty years. Daily, I had to keep walking. I had the faith. My faith account had to be deposited into everyday, without faith, my works are in vain.

Deuteronomy 29:3-6 NIV

With your own eyes you saw those great trials, those signs and great wonders. But this day the Lord has not given you a mind that understands or eyes that see or ears that hear. Yet the Lord says, "During the forty years that I led you through the wilderness, your clothes did not wear out, nor did the sandals on your feet. You ate no bread and drank no wine or other fermented drink. I did this so that you might know that I am the Lord your God.

Everyday, God provided a new provision and

strength to meet my goals. Daily progress was inevitable. Although I could not see it, I did realize it at every milestone. Those in the wilderness did not realize their shoes or clothing did not wear out until their release.

When therapy began, I could not rely on the energy or the success I had the day before. Each day presented new challenges and a fresh faith. I was not able to take the strength I had from the day before and think oh, well I did it yesterday, and I will just rely on that.

Just as these children were not allowed to store away manna for the next day, I too had to rely on God for a new refreshing and strength every day. Where God guides, He provides.

Daily application

Allow God to lead you. Trust His guidelines, if He tells you put nothing away until tomorrow, be obedient. The provision is already in place.

Day 15

Tie up that shoe

Philippians 3:1 NIV

Repetition is a vital part of any kind of therapy. When it came to each therapy, I did not seem to have an issue with this. The frustration came when I re-learned a task so simple, tying my shoes. Every day, I attempted and was unsuccessful. Finally, my occupational therapist said she would be getting me shoes with the velcro straps if I did not tie them. Funny enough, the next attempt I tied my shoelaces. I did not want those shoes; I told her they would cramp my style.

I am unsure what was going on here. In the beginning, I really could not lace my shoes again. I do not know if had silently given up or if I was tired of trying. Clearly, the task was in me all along. I just needed that extra push.

Philippians 3:1 NIV

Furthermore, my brothers and sisters, rejoice in the

Lord! It is no trouble for me to write the same things to you again, and it is a safeguard for you.

Repetition is beneficial. Proof is right here in Philippians 3:1. God is pleased when His children come to Him in need of boosts to keep going. One of our many duties as followers of Christ is commitment. All aspects of life require commitment; career, education, health journeys, and most of all giving our lives to Christ.

Even though some tasks seem minor, like tying shoelaces. The greater portion of the process, commitment, is the valuable lesson at hand. No matter how strenuous your commitment process may be, remember you are not troubling God when you seek His guidance regardless of often you ask.

Daily Application

Choose to be committed to anything you face that is for your betterment and growth in Christ. He is already available an infinite amount of times, all you have to do is seek.

Day 16

Familiar or Not

Colossians 3:1-2 NKJV

Have you ever been somewhere that you have been before, but it is not the same? Confusing, right? Well, I had this experience during my release from the hospital. When I learned I was going home, I did not want to go. So many thoughts plagued my mind. What was I supposed to do without around the clock care? Even though nurses coming and going out of my hospital room every hour was aggravating, it was concrete.

The new, old place I was returning to called home had the potential to pose many challenges. Those challenges could have turned into difficulties and burdens if I allowed them. The biggest obstacles I still faced were low, cloudy vision and limited mobility. I could not get up in the middle of the night alone, nor could I move at any time during the day on my own. Help, help, help was my constant.

Colossians 3:1-2 NKJV

If then you were raised with Christ, seek those things which are above, where Christ is, sitting at the right hand of God. Set your mind on things above, not on things on the earth.

A carnal mindset has not worked for me throughout this journey; neither will it work during any season of transition. During this season, I did not want the next chapter, returning home. I grew comfortable in the hospital.

God gave me no choice but to move from one place to another. Moving from the hospital to home took me from one type of mindset to another. I learned the importance of a transitional mindset. Shifting away from a carnal mindset, looking at what is into a Christ like mindset, focused on what will be.

Daily Application

Identify a mindset shift needed in your life. Recognize it, journal it, and pray to God for guidance and direction in your new step forward.

__Day 17__

Again?

Matthew 6:8-13 KJV

While I was learning to write again, one of my therapists had me write something I knew verbatim to ensure a constant writing flow. I would say that I subconsciously selected the Lord's Prayer, however, I know it was God.

It wasn't until quite sometime after therapy when my mom found notebooks full of the Lord's Prayer written over and over that I was reminded of the power of the Lord's Prayer in my life.

She asked if I remembered when we said the Lord's Prayer whenever I had a seizure. My response, "no I don't ". This is one of those full circle moments and a true confirmation of Deuteronomy 31:6 NIV, "Be strong and courageous. Do not be afraid or terrified because of them, for the Lord your God goes with you, he will never leave you nor forsake you".

God never left, a season of the Lord's prayer passed, another season of the Lord's Prayer came.

Daily Application

Have no fear when the same Word reappears. It is one of the many ways God speaks to us and reminds everyone of His presence. When God's word ceased my seizures, His power showed. When this Word developed my handwriting His might, power and promise came to assure me of His presence.

Today, seek God in places where He has met you before. If you hear a word from Him that you have before, do not dismiss it, dig into and find purpose.

Day 18

Are you tired yet?

Genesis 4:6 NKJV

My seizures went away, what a blessing! Then, wait, what? They came back. I put in so much hard work; everything was moving along smooth. I found my rhythm, knew when to rest and when to go. What in the world, was I to do with seizures...again? This was an unexpected and unwanted disruption, or so I thought.

Now, I entered a place, where even more was required of me than before. Early in 2012, a lot was required, but I did not even know I was in the world, so much so, I do not remember. The burden of gap filing laid on the prayer warriors, specifically my mother.

My countenance did fall, I grew sad and did not understand, another setback, why God? I had already grown tired, then refreshed, then tired, then spunky again. I even tried making sense of the occurrence myself, of course, that route was out of my hands, I tried it anyway.

Genesis 4:6 NKJV

Why has thou countenance fallen?

Daily Application

Why are you sad? Is there an area of your life where your countenance has fallen? What are things you can do to lift yourself up? Is it a setback or a setup? God does not cause anything that does not have a purpose. Has your countenance fallen? Is do, dive in God's word for a pick me up.

Day 19

Breathe life

Ezekiel 37:14 NKJV

All of the supernatural healing I experienced could only come from one place, God. There is no way I could overcome death and blindness. Only God can bring life back to the dead and heal blind eyes. God put His spirit in me throughout my entire ordeal. He continues to daily.

When I began to realize God put His spirit in me, it was not early during my hospital stay. In fact, it was a few years after. Every day I found myself desiring more of Him. My commitment to God grew so deep; there was not a day that went by where I did not call on Him. There were moments I unintentionally found myself reading His word and talking to Him. My new life routine centered around God.

Ezekiel 37:14 NKJV

I will put my spirit in you, and you shall live, and I

will place you in your own land. Then you shall know that, I the Lord, have spoken it and performed it, says the Lord.

Daily Application

God put His spirit in me, and the divine plan He has for my life began to unfold. As I gave myself to Him, I started to live on His terms, following His directions. He promised me life. He spoke it and orchestrated it. All with my obedience: and His plan. Are you open for God to place His spirit in you, so you will live and thrive?

Day 20

Level up

John 1:16 NKJV

Seasons changed, chapters changed, levels changed, and so did my steps of grace. Grace is a gift that only comes from God. Being committed to every phase of my God given journey is my priority. For my diligence, God consistently blessed me with grace upon grace. Grace is a pleasing word, yet has a great demand.

By definition, grace means the manifestation of favor. The demand of grace requires full surrender to God and giving Him nothing short of your best. For me, this meant deepening my commitment to the task before me.

I yearned for miracles to happen for me daily. This may sound selfish to some, when I clearly understood that it is God's desire to bless me and for me to live an abundant life full of blessings, I asked Him for everything. I also knew that if I did not receive what I asked for right away that He is fully and completely able. After all, His timing is not mine, nor is it my doctors.

John 1:16 NKJV

And of His fullness we have all received, and grace for grace.

God given grace is one of many gifts He gives to His children, even when we do not deserve it. God graced me during my times of sadness, anger and wanting to give up. I knew I was rooted in Him; I just did not understand if He had left me or not, and if He did then why.

Every time I head into a rut, here comes God with another step of grace, another blessing, and confirmation. Always in constant overflow.

Daily Application

Examine yourself. Have you given up? God does not put any more on us than we can bear (1 Corinthians 10:13). Today, I encourage you to seek God for the tasks He has for you to experience the next level of grace in store for you.

Day 21

I am

Isaiah 41:10 KJV

I love God, I trust God, I have faith in God. Fear does not live in my house, but it has made a visit or two. Sometimes fear crept in on me and I did not realize it. Going to some doctor's visits, I needed a comforter, other times I needed peace, I needed whatever God could be in any given moment.

God is literally everything I need. In Isaiah 41:10, God makes a statement so profound; it gets my attention every time I hear it. Now that I am further along in my recovery, I understand what it means for God to be my "I am."

When an eye doctor told me, my vision would not get better and she did not need to see me again, I burst into tears and boldly stated "I do not receive that". She left the exam room, so did my family and I.

It wasn't until years later, as my roots grew deeper in God, that I understood my boldness in that moment. That is an appointment I will never forget.   There was something unexplainable brewing inside of me. It was another step of faith.

I was typically not this bold and expressive in my faith. Whatever report I was given, I took it, cried about it and prayed privately. Along this road, I never fully realized the different types of fear I experienced.   What I do know is, God has consistently been the "I am" during every season.

He always said, Tiffany, why are you crying, I am your comforter.   Tiffany, why are you frustrated, I am your peace, Tiffany why are you quiet, talk to Me, I am your friend. There has been no reason to fear. Anytime I tried to operate in fear, God stepped in and reminded me, that He is the great "I am."

Isaiah 41:10 KJV

Fear not for I am with you.

In Isaiah 41:10 God is speaking from a place of gentleness to provide comfort to His people in captivity. The declaration "fear not" is bold, but it comes with peace. "Fear not", in a fearful situation surely stands out.

"I do not receive that", a bold statement I made, but yet it was saturated with the peace of

God, despite the report I received.

Daily Application

Pursue God to be your divine "I am".

Day 22

Good Tears

Jeremiah 31:9 NLT

Tears of joy, tears of pain, tears of excitement, tears of accomplishment, and tears of sadness, I have cried them all. Of all of these, the tears of joy hold a special kind of feeling. Crying can be mistaken for sadness. Even when I cried happy tears, I did so in private. This helped me avoid any conversation that might lead to even more crying. Another level of growth took place for me to completely understand different stages of emotions, and that my emotions are just that, mine.

I experienced several phases of emotional transition. When I received not so pleasing news, my growth allowed me to put aside my personal feelings quicker than before. This process helped me realize that new levels required new demands, and that these demands were not always spiritual, physical or mental. They were also emotional. Understanding tears of joy took me some time. Once I did understand, I was still afraid to shed them.

Jeremiah 31:9 NLT

Tears of joy will stream down their faces, and I will lead them home with great care. They will walk beside streams and on smooth paths where they will not stumble.

Daily Application

Another pivotal moment presented itself. These tears of joy were confirmation that God remained with me. He promised to lead me through this journey by way of His guidance and His way.

Trust the way God has prepared for you, cry those tears and should you stumble, know that stumbling with God is still part of the divine plan for your life. Count your Godly stumbles as blessings.

Day 23

Rooted

Ephesians 3:17-19 NKJV

God did not only create me to be blessed, His purpose is also for me to live in the blessings. This meant that I had to understand the timing God has on each phase of my journey. Every step of the way and every doctors' report brought along some form of blessings, whether the result was what I wanted or not. Learning not to classify a report as good or bad is a significant part of my path.

Instead, the strategy I learned to apply involved me receiving information, understanding the diagnosis and treatment plans. Next, I had to seek spiritual guidance to apply God's word accurately. The word of God reads the same straight from the page every time, the receiving, application and living the Word varies from person to person and situation to situation.

Living in blessings required the same attention and commitment to being rooted in God every time. Since I am dedicated to the life God has for me, I choose to implement any strategy He requires. When a doctor told me that my vision would not progress even though there was healing taking place, I activated an intangible faith. Faith in the unseen, which requires deep roots, I cried, told her I did not receive that. I relied on the roots of my faith.

In this moment, and days to follow I did not realize how much I had grown in God until my faith was put to test in that short moment. The doctor gave me her results, I gave her mine, she told me I did not need to come back, then left the office. This whirlwind moment set the pace for the trajectory of my recovery.

Ephesians 3:17-19 NKJV

That Christ may dwell in your hearts through faith; that you, being rooted in love, may be able to comprehend with all the saints what is the width and length and depth and height. To know the love of Christ which passes knowledge; that you may be filled with all the fullness of God.

This is a portion of Paul's prayer to God for the Ephesians. For me, this is a display of God's work when someone is put into isolation. I have never been in isolation. Though I have had plenty of productive alone time with God, like Paul. God will place you where you need to be, so that He can do His most intimate work on you. If you are like Paul, it may be in prison. If you are like me, it may be through a medical issue.

However, God needs to get your attention, He will. Then He will mold and shape you as your roots grow deeper and deeper. Paul found himself in God, grew strong in his faith and desired for people to share his same personal experience with Christ.

Daily Application

Allow your roots to deepen through faith. The deeper the roots, the stronger, and more secure are the blessings that follow. As a tree grows upward, its roots develop at new depths. Each step works together for the future good of the tree. The same came about in my life, the more I grew in His word, the stronger my faith became.

A trees roots are isolated like Paul was. If God takes you away from the life you know, be prepared for the unimaginable. That's the God we serve.

Day 24

Where's David?

1 Samuel 17 NLT

We all have a David spirit in us and believe me, it comes out just when you need it. Like David, during my journey, I did not intend on facing these giants of life support, brain injury, blindness and epilepsy. These are battles God had set aside specifically for me.

Why me and why this battle? Only God knows. I can firmly stand on the fact that God sent this battle to reveal the David in me and not to give attention to the Goliath's I encounter along the way.

Yes, the giants I face are huge, just like the Philistines, but so is my slingshot. There is no fancy way for me to dress up to slay these giants daily. The armor David attempted to wear did not fit him, it was too heavy, awkward, big and uncomfortable.

David went into battle in the name of God, which is all he needed to defeat Goliath, the massive Philistine.

1 Samuel 17 NLT

Daily application

It is already written that trials and tests are coming all of our ways. In these days, we have already been warned through God's word.

Today, I challenge you to prepare to your slingshot and catapult at any giants you encounter.

Spend your time with God reading 1 Samuel chapter 17 and see yourself as David.

Day 25

More than a conqueror
Romans 8:37 NIV

I take this journey one day at a time and I stand on the fact that this portion of my story is not the end of my story.

A day that has passed by is now behind me, the day upon me is filled with moments for now and tomorrow has not arrived, but will also be a day passed that too, is now behind me.

I have been asked how I got through this journey and how am I continuing to get through it, the answer is simple, though the action may be hard, one day at a time, like the children in the wilderness for 40 years. I have no control over my healing, recovery or timing. What I do have control over is my faith and commitment.

There is no portion of my God given journey that is in vain. It is my duty as His servant to share every part of my testimony. While I was in consistent prayer throughout the journey of this work, I heard God say clearly, "the kingdom needs your entire testimony."

The kingdom needs to know the cause of my blood clots was birth control. The kingdom needs to know I shed so many tears in hurt, pity, sadness and shame. The kingdom needs to know I have bad days just like I have good ones.

Now, I shed those same tears to rejoice, celebrate and testify to becoming a conqueror.

Romans 8:37 NIV

No, in all these things we are more than conquerors through Him who loved us.

Daily Application

More than a conqueror is who I am. It is also who you are. Even when days seem hard, take note to the tasks you have overcome in that day. No one task is bigger than another. Anything you face, conquer it head on.

Lifeline closing prayer

Father God, to each and every hand this devotional passes through, I pray supernatural healing in any area of their life where they yearn for more of You. Every person, every testimony, everything You do has a unique, specific plan attached to it. I made it my goal to seek You first, after stumbling on my own multiple times, You remained faithful to me and waited patiently for me. In closing, I ask that You bless, cover and direct the paths of each soul who has joined me on this Lifeline journey.

Amen

Notes

ABOUT THE AUTHOR

Tiffany is a faithful servant and child of God. She was only 26 years old when her life changed in 2012. Her drastic, personal encounter with death and God sets the tone for the next phase of her life.

Before the injury, she lived life on her own as a paralegal. The legal field is Tiffany's career passion. Now she knows her only job is working for the Great One.

Today, Tiffany shares her testimony every chance she gets. So, watch out, you may leave a conversation with her feeling free, serving God and seeking out your life's purpose.

Tiffany's recovery is moving steadily along. Although she lives with epilepsy caused by the initial brain injury, she does not allow her limitations to keep her from doing what she loves, which is spreading God's word through her powerful testimony.

Made in the USA
Coppell, TX
20 November 2019